Representational Monetary Identity

The System of Monetary Crisis

First Edition

April 16, 2013

Representational Monetary Identity

Copyright ©① 2013 Mirelo Deugh Ausgam Valis

Published by Lulu, Inc. (lulu.com), 2013

ISBN: 978-1-105-18867-1

Cover image © Anton Balazh - Fotolia.com

To those who produce our wealth

The Author

Mirelo Deugh Ausgam Valis is a pseudonym.

Contents

Preface	i
Introduction	1
The Problem	3
The Solution	4
Money	5
Possible Money	7
Nothingness	8
Omnistitution	11
Money as Multiequivalence	12
Money as Omniequivalence	15
Nongeneric Omniequivalence	21
Actual Money	29
Relative Exchange Value	31
Monetary Value	35
Monetary Representation	41
Representational Monetary Value	44
Fractional-Reserve Banking	46
Conclusion	49
Bibliography	51

Preface

This book is the product of a world undergoing an international monetary crisis. Its aim is to identify a single, necessary, and sufficient cause of the current or any other such crisis. For Marx, that single cause was a struggle between social classes. For us, it is quite something else.

In this investigation, despite confirming various discoveries by Marx, we will find critical flaws in his conceptualization of them. Yet Marx was not alone in his guilt for those flaws: he was just unable to transcend certain prejudices deeply and long embedded in monetary philosophy.

Because of those prejudices, Marx mistook, for example, what he called commodity "Fetishism" for a feature of all money and any priced commodities, thus compromising his own discovery.

This investigation will begin precisely with commodity "Fetishism," or as I preferably call it, "representational monetary identity" (the title of this book), which means to confuse money with its representation. Once no longer inherently monetary, this confusion becomes that ultimate source of monetary crisis we aim to identify. However, to learn why socially distinguishing money from its representation must alone deactivate the system of monetary crisis, or how to achieve that, we must overcome the same philosophical prejudices that victimized Marx and continue to victimize almost all monetary thinking.

Still, which are those prejudices, and what causes them?

As will become evident, they always consist in mistaking the actuality of money for its mere possibility. Along this investigation, many such mistakenly timeless, unchangeable money forms will collapse while we understand monetary identity, first as generic, then as representational.

Yet before investigating representational monetary identity, we must somehow illustrate it, which we will do right away, by analyzing the process of banks loaning a fraction from their clients' account balances to other clients than its original depositors while keeping the remainder as reserves—fractional reserve banking.

Introduction

According to the Federal Reserve Bank of Chicago, this is how fractional-reserve banking originated:

> Then, bankers discovered that they could make loans merely by giving their promises to pay, or bank notes, to borrowers. In this way, banks began to create money. [Nic94]

There was also the need, however—as there always is—of keeping, at any given time, enough money to provide for expected withdrawals: "Enough metallic money had to be kept on hand, of course, to redeem whatever volume of notes was presented for payment" [Nic94].

Hence the name "fractional-reserve banking": commercial banks must hold a *fraction* of all deposit money as *reserves*—which legally (since 1971) are no longer valuable as gold but only as a *public debt*—to provide for expected withdrawals: "Under current regulations, the reserve requirement against most transaction accounts is 10 percent" [Nic94].

In the fractional-reserve banking system, on which most of today's international monetary system relies, commercial banks create money by *loaning* it, hence as a *private debt*.

> Transaction deposits are the modern counterpart of bank notes. It was a small step from printing notes to making book entries crediting deposits of borrowers, which the borrowers in turn could "spend" by writing checks, thereby "printing" their own money. [Nic94]

For example, if a commercial bank receives a new deposit of $10,000.00, then 10% of this new deposit becomes the bank's reserves for loaning up to $9,000.00 (the 90% in excess of reserves), with interest. Likewise, if a loan of that maximum fraction of $9,000.00 does occur and the borrower also deposits it into a bank—regardless of whether in the same bank or not—then again 10% of it becomes the latter bank's reserves for loaning now up to $8,100.00 (the 90% now in *excess reserves*), always with interest. This could proceed indefinitely, adding $90,000.00 to the money supply, valuable only as their borrowers' resulting debt: after endless loans of recursively smaller 90% fractions from the original deposit of $10,000.00, that same deposit would have eventually become the 10% reserves for itself as a total of $100,000.00.[1]

> Thus through stage after stage of expansion, "money" can grow to a total of 10 times the new reserves supplied to the banking system, as the new deposits created by loans at each stage are added to those created at all earlier stages and those supplied by the initial reserve-creating action. [Nic94]

Now let us further examine what is happening here. First, we have a deposit. Then, we have a loan of up to a fraction (of 90%) of this deposit. Finally, the borrower can deposit the borrowed money into another bank account, in the same bank or not. Suddenly, the trillion dollar question emerges: is the borrowed money in these two bank accounts *the same*?

- On the one hand, the answer is yes: all borrowed money came from the original deposit—so it is that same original money.

- On the other hand, the answer is no: all money deposited into the borrower's account possibly stays in the original depositor's account—so it is not that same original money.

How can that be?

Let us consider gold instead of bank accounts. Gold at once *is* and *represents* money. It *is* money by being its own social equivalence to all commodities, and so the generic exchange value in their price. It *represents* money by being the object in which all commodities must be priced, whether valuable or worthless in itself (independently of being money). Whatever we choose for the representation of money—whether valuable in itself or not—it must be socially identical to all commodities in their exchange value, or in their equivalence to it and to each other in it. This general equivalence is *monetary identity*, which is purely abstract. Yet money must also be an object, like gold, possibly a commodity with its own exchange value, again like gold: the object in which to price all commodities. This object is a *monetary representation*, which is not only concrete (like gold), but also replaceable—say, as gold by silver.

---

[1] After sixty recursive loans of 0.9 excess in reserves each, a $10,000.00 deposit would have already become $10,000.00 $\times \frac{1 - 0.9^{60}}{1 - 0.9} = \$99,820.29897\ldots$

The Problem

So let us go back to fractional-reserve banking. Now, by conceptually distinguishing money from its representation, we can clearly see what is happening in that ambiguous loaning from bank deposits: commercial banks are mistaking bank accounts for the money they represent. This way, when they deposit a loan from any account into any other, they must mistake the same loan for both accounts, hence *duplicating* its money, rather than *subtracting* it from the source account. That confusion between monetary identity (deposit money) and its representation (bank accounts) is thus what alone *replicates* loaned money: two deposits in different accounts must always be different money, even if one is just a loan of money from the other.

The same confusion affects a variety of monetary representations, like paper notes and metal coins. Even when sheer gold represents money, there is no inherent distinction between monetary identity and its representation. Any such inherent indistinction (confusion) is precisely what I call *representational monetary identity*.

With no representational identity of money, not a single fraction of bank-account balances could belong to both its depositors and their borrowers. As *account* money, deposits from loans are new money. However, as *deposit* money, they are just fractions of other account balances. Hence banks lacking up to 90% of all money their clients can withdrawal: bank loans are just bank-account money that vanishes once repaid.

Additionally, because all money created by commercial banks is just a sum of balance fractions borrowed from client accounts, that money must be worth only as *credit*, or as the corresponding debt *principal*. This way, except for money not yet in loans nor else reserved—whether in bank accounts (excess reserves) or not—but not from loans, bank loans are the whole money supply left for paying their own interest. Consequently, such an interest-paying, self-indebted money supply must grow at least at its own interest rate less any other money off the banks' reserves.

Then, who should create the additional money? Supposedly, governments would do it. Yet historically, central banks have been issuing most of this money in exchange for promises from their governments of paying it back with interest, just like commercial banks replicate it in exchange for promises from their clients of paying it back with interest. So paying the additional interest (that on public money-as-debt) requires even more money: central banks must create—and are creating—ever new public money-as-debt for paying interest on both private and old public money-as-debt, thus recursively amplifying the problem.

The Solution

In both this exposition and the world, we can already see the disastrous consequences of such a monetary system, with its limitless, exponential growth of the money supply as a debt—first private, then public. We have a problem: *debt* becoming *money*. What is the solution? The answer comes from understanding the problem: since to create irrational, self-multiplying money we must confuse monetary identity with its representation, the solution is to disentangle them.

By which not even gold money, for having as much a representational identity as that of bank accounts, is immune to its own self-indebtedness. Indeed, it was by creating proxy representations of monetary gold that fractional-reserve banking originally flourished. The reason is that—as we will see—with any monetary proxies of gold, its representational monetary identity must become a debt.

Hence the advent of central banking: because monetary gold proxies are already a debt, all additional such money, even if public, must be borrowed. So any public-debt-free, government-issued monetary proxies of gold, for not solving the money-as-private-debt problem, could only postpone the money-as-public-debt one.

Still, if the only solution to the whole (both public and private) money-as-debt problem is an inherently distinct monetary identity, then how to implement it?

Fortunately, an already existing monetary system inherently distinguishes monetary identity from its representation: the Bitcoin monetary system.[2] It uses public-key cryptography (the same technology of private Internet connections) to implement monetary identity as a private key and its representation as the corresponding public key, so this representation becomes inherently distinct from its represented money. The whole Bitcoin system relies on that distinction: as an essentially decentralized monetary system, it controls the money supply by self-certifying a public chain of monetary transactions, which contains money representations (public keys) alone, and never the money (private keys) they represent. This way, monetary identity remains nonrepresentational, private, possibly anonymous (pseudonymous), and impossible to replicate.

Yet in case Bitcoin eventually fails, any other solutions, not only to the money-as-public-debt problem, but also to the underlying money-as-private-debt one, must also consist in distinguishing monetary identity from its representation.

---

[2] By "Bitcoin," I mean the Bitcoin system's architecture, as outlined in "Bitcoin: A Peer-to-Peer Electronic Cash System" (http://bitcoin.org/bitcoin.pdf).

Money

> Reason has always existed, but not always in a reasonable form.
>
> Karl Marx

We must begin with the concept of *representational monetary identity*: the confusion between monetary identity and its representation. By this concept, money has two dimensions:

1. It is its *identity* to the social exchange value of all commodities (its own social equivalence to them), or the generic exchange value in their price. This priced value depends on its own representation by an object—just as deposit money depends on bank accounts—which makes monetary identity purely abstract—or subjective, like deposit money. That abstractness is all that makes balance fractions lent between different accounts *identical* deposit money: abstract money is just its own exchange value. Indeed:

   > So far no chemist has ever discovered exchange value either in a pearl or a diamond. [Mar67]

2. It is its *representation* in prices (of commodities), by an object. This pricing object is independent of its represented money—just as bank accounts are independent of deposit money—which makes monetary representations concrete—or objective, like bank accounts.[3] That concreteness is all that makes balance fractions lent between different accounts *different* deposit money: a concrete money (gold, silver, paper notes, metal coins, bank accounts, or any other object) is just its own representation.

---

[3] Only concrete objects can represent something without depending on it.

Knowing the difference between monetary identity and its representation constitutes a new, dual concept of money, while confusing them reproduces its old, unilateral—either objective or subjective—concept. However, completely accepting the new concept depends on answering: how can its two monetary dimensions, one (the priced value) purely abstract and the other (the pricing object) always concrete, ever become one same thing, as they do in the unity of each *price*?[4]

This is the same old, philosophical question Descartes faced regarding the soul and the body (although supposedly money has no soul): how could an immaterial thing coexist with a material one, to Descartes in us—to us in money? We now can give an original answer to that question, by explaining how monetary identity and its representation can coexist in the single entity we call money.

---

[4]Bank accounts can only be pricing objects by meaning their own *fractional balances*.

Possible Money

Nothing can be the social exchange value of all commodities—their equivalence to it and so to each other in it—without quantifying itself, by being its own concretely quantitative, objective representation. Conversely, nothing can represent its own social equivalence to all commodities—the generic exchange value in their price—without again quantifying itself, by being now its own abstractly quantitative, represented money. This way, a pure abstraction and a concrete object must become each other.

Yet how could it happen?

Whenever we conceive of abstractions externally, they become concrete. For example, I can imagine a price evaluation as resulting from someone else's brain processes. I can even imagine each of my own price evaluations as resulting from its corresponding brain processes, as if it were someone else's abstraction. However, I cannot imagine my own abstractions while still performing them: no conscious act of imagination can be to this consciousness the object of another such act by the same consciousness, at the same time. Hence, no price evaluation could be the result of any brain processes to whom at the same time performs it, always requiring instead another act of imagination—by someone else or in a different time—to make it a concrete, imaginable object. Likewise, this new act of imagination could itself only become a concrete, imaginable object with yet another such act—always by a different consciousness or in a different time.

If this infinite regression were to govern the relation between abstract and concrete money, then we would be condemned to direct exchange. On the contrary, the abstract exchange value of money must rather be concrete as also its quantifying, representing object, which in turn must rather be abstract as also its quantified, represented monetary value.

However, pure abstractions are nothing concrete, while concrete objects are nothing abstract: money as just an exchange value must be nothing of the object representing it, and money as just an object must be nothing of the monetary value it represents. Therefore, as always *both* an exchange value *and* an object, at the same time, for everyone, money (as *either* an exchange value *or* an object) requires its own absence (as respectively an object and an exchange value): it must (as either one) be nothing (as the other). Then, by being at all times, for everyone, as much an abstract exchange value as a concrete object, the presence of money becomes its absence: being becomes nothingness.

Consequently, at least regarding money, being and nothingness are the same.

Nothingness

The idea of nothingness as being something, perhaps even everything, may seem an absurdity. However, by definition:

1. Nothingness is the absence of something, possibly of everything.

2. If anything is absent, then:

    (a) Its presence is *nothing*.
    (b) The nothingness of its presence is *present*.

Then, because being present requires being *something*—a *being*—nothingness must have a being that, in the absence of everything, would itself be everything.

Being as Nothingness

In 1901, Bertrand Russell discovered the following paradox:

> *As a barber, a citizen shaves all and only citizens who do not shave themselves: does that barber shave himself?*

If he does, then he no longer shaves *only* citizens who do not shave themselves, by shaving a citizen (himself) who shaves himself. And if he does not, then he no longer shaves *all* citizens who do not shave themselves, by not shaving a citizen (himself) who does not shave himself.

Generalizing to any other scenario, a set of all and only self-exclusive sets must include itself to include *all* self-exclusive sets, and must exclude itself to include *only* self-exclusive sets.[5]

Mathematicians have proposed many solutions to this paradox, one of which became the now-canonical set theory by Zermelo and Fraenkel. However, none of those or any other mathematical theories could let a set include all sets. This is because a set including all sets must include itself, allowing us to exclude it from itself by excluding from it all and only self-inclusive sets. Which would make the original set no longer self-exclusive (because no longer self-inclusive), then again self-exclusive (because again self-inclusive), thus already reproducing the paradox.

Even so, there is at least one of such possibly—hence possibly not yet—paradoxical sets: the concept of "everything," which by definition must include all sets, despite being one of them. For including itself as

---

[5]Symbolically, if we let $R = \{x \mid x \notin x\}$, then $R \in R \Leftrightarrow R \notin R$.

a consequence of including all sets, that concept lets Russell's paradox assume this absolute form: would "everything self-exclusive" (everything not self-inclusive) be a self-exclusive concept?

As thus, overcoming this paradox requires the concept of "everything" to either be meaningless or false, or else identical to that of "nothingness," this way requiring us in turn to analyze each one of these possibilities individually:

1. If "everything" were just a meaningless concept, then it would be posing us no paradox: like any other word, "everything" can only become paradoxical as a *meaning*, whether this meaning is false or identical to that of "nothingness."

2. If "everything"—which can only mean *all beings*[6]—were false, then *each being* would also be false.[7] Consequently:

    (a) Being and nothingness would be the same.
    (b) Either being or nothingness would be both false as itself and true as respectively nothingness and being.
    (c) The concept of "everything" would be identical to that of "nothingness," as in the only other alternative left.

3. And so, the concept of "everything" is both true and false, by being identical to that of "nothingness."

The result is that being and nothingness are the same.

Truth as Falsehood

Hence the prototype of all paradoxes:

This statement is false.

If that statement is true, then for its assertion of its own falsity to be true, it must be false. However, if the same statement is false, then for its assertion of its own falsity to be false, it must be true. So "this statement is false" must not only be false, whenever true, but also true, whenever false: truth and falsehood must be the same.

Indeed, even if being and nothingness are the same, the truth of each one still means the falsity of the other, so truth and falsehood must also be the same.

---

[6]Likewise, the set of all sets can only mean *all sets*.
[7]The meaninglessness of "everything," instead of causing its *falsity*, would *prevent* it: only a *meaning* can be false.

Being from Nothingness

Ultimately, nothingness is in itself identical to being:

1. Nothingness is not *any* single being: whenever I choose a single being, it will be different from nothingness.

2. Nothingness is not *every* single being: whenever I choose all beings, each one will be different from nothingness.[8]

Either definition is complete without the other: nothingness is *indifferently* not any or not every single being. Indeed, "not any single being" results the same as "not every single being," despite meaning different procedures. However, if *not any* single being is *not every* single being, then *any* being is identical to *every other* being. Hence, any being is different from itself in every possible way: it never has its own being, which yet is the only being it can have. So each being is—or all beings are—nothing: being and nothingness are the same.

Nothingness from Being

Conversely, being is in itself identical to nothingness:

1. Being is *each* being: any and every partial, relative being.

2. Being is *all* beings: their total, absolute being.[9]

Either definition is *incomplete* without the other: being is *both* each being *and* all beings. Indeed, the being of each relative part of all beings and that of their absolute totality depend and result on each other.[10] However, no partial, relative being is a total, absolute being: each single being is not all beings. Therefore, being is either each one or the totality of all beings: it cannot be both, which yet are nothing without each other. So being is neither each single being nor the totality of all beings, hence is nothing: being and nothingness are—again—the same.

---

[8]The word "every" means both "all" and "each," or "all *as* each": by saying "not every being" to mean "some but not other beings," I restrict the meaning of "every" to that of "all," as does the word "everything" (all beings). To prevent that, I must make the meaning of "each" explicit in "every," by rather saying "not every *single* being."

[9]Like the set of all sets, the being of all beings includes itself.

[10]It is precisely because *each* being depends on *all* beings that we cannot conceptually abolish "everything" (all beings).

Omnistitution

Still, if nothingness is the contrary of being, which in turn is the contrary of nothingness, then how can they be the same? How is their mutual identity possible, if they define themselves, precisely, by opposing each other? Which common identity can solve this contradiction?

The answer must be something that, despite existing, does not exist—something that is also nothing. However, which being, despite being nothing, remains a being?

That being is the substitution of nothing by nothing. The self-substitution of nothingness is the only being always identical to its nothingness, as an absent substitution, which hence is always identical to that same being, as a present substitution. There is no other being like it:

1. Although the concept of "nothingness" is both nothing and a being as a meaning and a brain process, respectively, the same concept is not all beings that can be nothing in the meaning of which it is the brain process: the concept of "nothingness" is not all beings of which it can be the nothingness.

2. Although the number zero is both nothing and a being as the number of elements in the empty set and an element in the set of all numbers, respectively, the same number is not all beings that can be nothing in the set of which it is the number of elements: the number zero is not all beings of which it can be the nothingness.

In contrast, the substitution of nothing by nothing, as always identical to its nothingness, is all beings of which it can be the nothingness, hence all beings of which it can be the absence, then all beings. Indeed:

1. For any other being *not* to be a substitution, it must be the substitution of nothing by nothing, as thus its own absence, and so nothing.

2. For any other being to *be* a substitution, it must lastly substitute between two beings of which none is a substitution, then of which both are nothing, so it is also the substitution of nothing by nothing.

Hence, for being such an absolute substitution, the self-substitution of nothingness requires transforming "substitution" into another word, one built by replacing the Latin prefix "sub-" (under) in "substitution"—meaning "to stand under the defining determination of something else, or to cause that"—by the likewise Latin prefix "omni-" (all and each): the word "omnistitution"—meaning "to stand under the totality and each of all defining determinations, or to cause that."

Money as Multiequivalence

Money has many functions, including those of quantifying and storing exchange value. However, its most fundamental function, on which all the others depend, is to enable otherwise impossible commodity exchange. Hence, for us to identify the first requirements money satisfies, or the first problems it solves, we must begin with an exchange scenario free not only from any actual, complete forms of money, but even from any just possible or incomplete ones: direct exchange. Let us then imagine two owners A and B of commodities x and y, respectively, of whom A wants y and B wants x. With no money and no third commodity, the only way for both owners to obtain their desired commodities is directly from each other:

$A \dashrightarrow y$	$B \dashrightarrow x$
x	y
y	x

However, direct exchange poses two problems, either of which alone is enough to prevent it. One has a subjective nature:

1. To be exchangeable for each other, x and y must share the same exchange value.

2. It can happen that every exchangeable quantity of x has a different exchange value than any exchangeable quantity of y.

The other problem has an objective nature instead. Let us imagine (as on the facing page) three owners A, B, and C of commodities x, y, and z, respectively, of whom A wants y, B wants z, and C wants x. Direct exchange cannot give those three owners their desired commodities, none of which belongs to whom (x to B) wants the commodity owned by whom (z by C) wants it (wants x). Moneyless exchange now can only happen if one of those commodities becomes a *multiequivalent*: a simultaneous equivalent of its two equivalent commodities at least for the owner who neither wants nor owns it—whether the other two owners also know of this multiequivalence or not. For example, just by possibly owning z, A can exchange x for z with C as if already exchanging z for y with B, this way making z a multiequivalent (as asterisked):

$A \dashrightarrow y$	$B \dashrightarrow z$	$C \dashrightarrow x$
x	y	z^*
z^*	y	x
y	z	x

Yet any such individually handled multiequivalence poses its own pair of problems:

1. It enables conflicting indirect exchange strategies. For example, in the last scenario, A can still try to exchange x for z with C (as if already exchanging z for y with B) even with B simultaneously trying to exchange y for x with A (as if already exchanging x for z with C).

2. It not only allows again for all mutually exchangeable quantities of two commodities to have different exchange values, but also makes this more likely, for combining different pairs of commodities.

Fortunately, those two problems share the same solution, which is a single multiequivalent m becoming *social*, or *money*. Then, commodity owners can either exchange—sell—their commodities for m or exchange m for—buy—the commodities they want. For example, let us again imagine three owners A, B, and C of commodities x, y, and z, respectively, of whom A wants y, B wants z, and C wants x, yet who now only exchange their commodities for that m social multiequivalent (initially owned just by A):

$A \dashrightarrow y$	$B \dashrightarrow z$	$C \dashrightarrow x$
x, m	y	z
x, y	m	z
x, y	z	m
y, m	z	x

With social (rather than individual) multiequivalence:

1. There are always exactly two exchanges for each owner (one for selling and the other for buying, or else reversely), with any number of such owners, in a uniform chain.

2. All owners exchange a common (social) multiequivalent, which eventually returns to its original owner.

Additionally, with a social multiequivalent (money) divisible into identical, small enough units, even if all mutually exchangeable quantities of two commodities have different exchange values, these two commodities will remain mutually exchangeable. For example, let us imagine two commodities x and y valuable as one and two units of a social multiequivalent m, respectively—$x(1m)$ and $y(2m)$. Let us then assume their owners to be A of x and B of y who own also three m units—$3m$—each, of whom A wants y and B wants x, and who again only exchange their commodities for m units—x for $1m$ and y for $2m$:

$A \dashrightarrow y$	$B \dashrightarrow x$
$x(1m)$, $3m$	$y(2m)$, $3m$
$y(2m)$, $2m$	$x(1m)$, $4m$

Finally, with social multiequivalence thus making, as only money does, commodity exchange always possible, any social multiequivalent is money, which in turn is any form of social multiequivalence.

Money as Omniequivalence

The being of money must be identical to its nothingness:

1. Money must be both its own social multiequivalence and a socially multiequivalent object.

2. Any such object is nothing of its own social multiequivalence.

3. The social multiequivalence of that object is nothing of the same object.

Therefore, understanding money requires mapping it into the only being that itself causes its own identity to nothingness: omnistitution. Indeed, since the substitution of nothing by nothing (omnistitution) is both nothing and everything, it applies to all beings in their nothingness. Consequently, omnistitution must apply to any socially multiequivalent object (to money), since any such object makes its own social multiequivalence nothing and becomes nothing because of it.

However, if omnistitution is everything, then all it can apply to is itself. Consequently, applying omnistitution must be the same as just understanding it.

Still, as understanding something is answering questions about it, which questions are there to ask about omnistitution? There can only be these four: where; when; how, and why does nothing substitute for nothing? Of which the most fundamental is the fourth (Why does nothing substitute for nothing?), because its answer must explain all the answers given to the other three (Where, when, and how does nothing substitute for nothing?). Indeed, if the self-substitution of nothingness is everything, then asking why does it happen includes asking the same question Martin Heidegger famously regarded as the most fundamental of all philosophy: why is there something instead of nothing?

So let us ask it: why does nothing substitute for nothing?

In any substitution, the substitutive being must be different from the substituted one—even if just in its moment in time. Otherwise, any concept of a substitution becomes impossible: no conceivable substitution is an exception to that, whether the substituted and substitutive beings in it are nothing or something, so nothingness must also differ from itself, by which alone it can substitute for itself.

As indeed, nothingness does differ from itself:

1. It is always the absence of everything, hence of any substitution.

2. The absence of any substitution is always the substitution of nothing by nothing, being thus always the presence of that substitution instead of the absence of any substitution.

3. By which nothingness is always the presence of its own substitution for itself instead of the absence of any substitution, despite being always that absence.

Hence, nothingness is always different from itself, this way preventing the substitution of nothing by nothing from ever being impossible: even in the absence of any substitution as resulting from the absence of everything, nothingness can still substitute for itself, by remaining different from itself. Additionally:

1. Nothingness must always have already substituted for itself, by always having already been different from the nothingness to which it is identical: the substitution of nothing by nothing must always have been actual.

2. Nothingness must always have just possibly substituted for itself, by always having still been the absence of its own substitution by itself as resulting from the absence of everything: the substitution of nothing by nothing must always have been just possible.

So the substitution of nothing by nothing has always been and will always be both actual and just possible. Indeed, as a substitutive being, nothingness is an already actual substitute of its not yet substitutive self, being thus already identical to the whole substitution of nothing by nothing: it becomes identical to the actuality of that substitution. While, as a substituted being, nothingness is not yet a substitute of itself, being thus just possibly identical to the whole substitution of nothing by nothing: it remains identical to the mere possibility of that substitution.

Consequently, the substituted nothingness is just possible as both the substitutive one and the whole substitution of nothing by nothing, by still not being substitutive. While the substitutive nothingness is already actual as both the substituted one and the whole substitution of nothing by nothing, by already being substitutive.

Conversely, the whole self-substitution of nothingness can only have a being in its either actual or just possible, self-substitutive nothingness by being itself either substitutive (actual) or substituted (just possible). Indeed, the nothingness of being—that of any absent presence—must be just possible or substituted while the being of nothingness—that of any present absence—must already be actual or substitutive. As thus, for the self-substitution of nothingness to have its whole being in that same self-substitutive nothingness, it must either be just possible, as the substituted—absent—nothingness of being (nothing), or already actual, as the substitutive—present—being of nothingness (everything).

Additionally, since each single being—including that of all beings—is both nothing and the substitution of nothing by nothing, that same being must also be an either substituted or substitutive nothingness. If substitutive, it already substitutes for itself, being thus its own *already equivalent* nothingness. If substituted, it just possibly substitutes for itself, being thus its own *just possibly equivalent* nothingness.

Likewise,

1. Any commodity must be exchangeable for an equivalent one.

2. Equivalent commodities are only different, then only exchangeable, as merely concrete objects.

3. The exchange between merely concrete yet equivalent objects is either impossible or the same as its absence. Consequently,

    (a) Commodity exchange must substitute nothing by nothing.

    (b) Any single commodity must itself be identical to the absence of any equivalent one for which it is exchangeable, being thus an either just possible or already actual equivalent of itself, respectively as either substituted by or substitutive of such an equivalent nothingness, whether directly or indirectly.

Hence, except with indirect exchange, if a commodity cannot substitute for any other one directly, then:

1. It can only be a commodity by remaining possible.

2. It remains possible only by being a just possible equivalent of some other commodity, which then substitutes for it directly.

Conversely, and still without indirect exchange, if the same commodity cannot be substituted by any other one directly, then:

1. It can only be a commodity by becoming actual.

2. It becomes actual only by being an actual equivalent of some other commodity, which it then substitutes for directly.

This precisely confirms the modeling Karl Marx did of direct exchange in his *Capital*:

> 20 yards of linen = 1 coat, or
>
> 20 yards of linen are worth 1 coat.
>
> Here two different kinds of commodities evidently play two different parts. The linen expresses its value in the coat; the coat serves as the material in which that value is expressed. The former plays an active, the latter a passive, part. [Mar67]

Without indirect exchange, any substitutive commodity must be the substitutive nothingness, and any substituted commodity must be the substituted nothingness. In practice, the owner A of commodity x, whenever directly exchanging it for commodity y owned by B, views x as just possibly equivalent to y, which is hence its actual equivalent—x just possibly substitutes for y, which hence already substitutes for x:

A	B
x: for A, just possibly equivalent to (substituted by) y	y: for A, already equivalent to (substitutive of) x

Conversely, the owner B of commodity y, whenever directly exchanging it for commodity x owned by A, views y as just possibly equivalent to x, which is hence its actual equivalent—y just possibly substitutes for x, which hence already substitutes for y:

A	B
x: for B, already equivalent to (substitutive of) y	y: for B, just possibly equivalent to (substituted by) x

This way, always confirming Marx, no two commodities could be merely possible equivalents of—substituted by—each other, for the same owner, at the same time, or they would be rather actual equivalents of—substitutive of—each other, for that same owner, at that same time:

A	B
x: for A, just possibly equivalent to (substituted by) an y already equivalent to (substitutive of) x	y: for B, just possibly equivalent to (substituted by) an x already equivalent to (substitutive of) y

Additionally, no two commodities could be actual equivalents of—substitutive of—each other, for the same owner, at the same time, or they would be rather just possible equivalents of—substituted by—each other, for that same owner, at that same time:

A	B
x: for B, already equivalent to (substitutive of) an y just possibly equivalent to (substituted by) x	y: for A, already equivalent to (substitutive of) an x just possibly equivalent to (substituted by) y

Still, any actual equivalent must also be just possible: its being the substitutive nothingness makes it the actuality of its own substituted self as just possibly substitutive. So that same equivalent must be both just possible and already actual.

Yet how could an actual equivalent remain actual and, for the same owner, at the same time, be also just possible?

For the actual nothingness and its merely possible, substituted self to be the same substitutive nothingness, the resulting actual nothingness must substitute for a new just possible one. Otherwise, there would be no merely possible, substituted nothingness left—which by definition is impossible. However, this newly substitutive, actual nothingness and its newly substituted, just possible self must still be the same substitutive, actual nothingness, which hence must always again substitute for another, ever different, just possible nothingness:

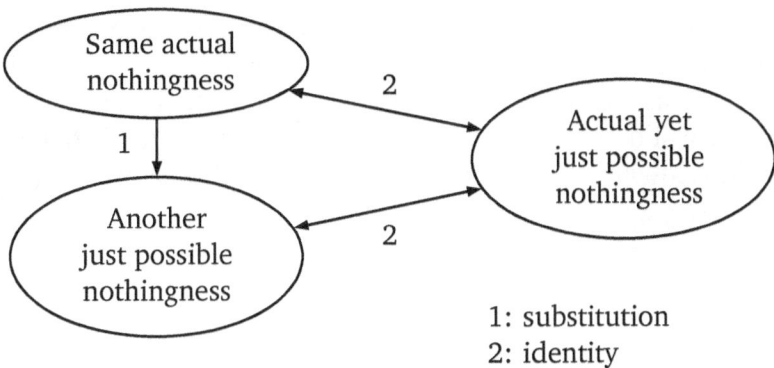

1: substitution
2: identity

And so, the only way any commodity can become, for the same owner, at the same time, both actual and just possible is by being the (actual) equivalent of all its (just) possible equivalents:

A	B (or B, C)
x: equivalent of all its possible equivalents	y: possible equivalent of x z: possible equivalent of x

Despite still calling this multiple equivalence "multiequivalence," from now on I will preferably call it "omniequivalence," which is the only word already having these two meanings:

1. It names actual yet just possible equivalence, or *generic* equivalence.

2. It names equivalence to all equivalents, or *general* equivalence.

The mere possibility of an omniequivalent no longer belongs to its merely possible equivalents, but rather to that omniequivalent itself. Therefore, any omniequivalent is absolute, rather than relative, in its actual equivalence, which now contains its own mere possibility. So its merely possible equivalents are also absolute, rather than relative, in their merely possible equivalence, which now is already actual as their absolute equivalent.

Relative Equivalence	
Actual equivalence	Just possible equivalence

Absolute Equivalence	
Actual yet just possible equivalence	Just possible equivalence

Additionally, as omniequivalence is always equivalence of single to multiple objects, an individual omniequivalent is any omniequivalent used in isolation by a single owner—an individual multiequivalent—while a social omniequivalent is any omniequivalent used in agreement by multiple owners—a social multiequivalent—also known as money.

Nongeneric Omniequivalence

Although the concepts of omniequivalence and multiequivalence both include the general aspect of money (as the equivalent of all equivalents), only that of omniequivalence includes its generic aspect (as an absolute, both actual and just possible equivalent), by mapping it into omnistitution—which will be essential to understanding representational monetary identity. Indeed, for having no concept of omniequivalence yet, Marx could only conceive of money as the generic "form" of a merely "general" monetary value:

> All commodities now express their value (1) in an elementary form, because in a single commodity; (2) with unity, because in one and the same commodity. This form of value is elementary and the same for all, therefore general. [Mar67]

However, since equivalence to all equivalents must be absolute, or both actual and just possible, there is no general equivalence that is not also generic. Hence the ambiguity of "omniequivalence" as indistinctly meaning two distinct equivalences, of which:

1. *Generic* equivalence is the absolute, both actual and just possible equivalence of either money or an individual omniequivalent to *each* of its multiple, just possible equivalents. A generic equivalent is *distinctly* actual and just possible:

    (a) An *actual* generic equivalent is an equivalent of *any* of its multiple, just possible equivalents. For example, if gold is already an equivalent of *each* commodity—whether socially (as money) or individually—then it must already be an equivalent of linen.

    (b) A *just possible* generic equivalent is an equivalent of *every other* than any of its multiple, just possible equivalents. For example, if gold is already an equivalent of linen—whether socially (as money) or individually—then it remains a just possible equivalent of *every other* commodity than linen.

2. *General* equivalence is the both actual and just possible equivalence of either money or an individual omniequivalent to *all* of its multiple, just possible equivalents. A general equivalent is *indistinctly* actual and just possible.

The only way one can see no difference between those meanings is by confusing actual equivalence with its mere possibility. This is the only way by which:

1. There is no possible difference between equivalence that is *both* actual *and* just possible, hence absolute, and equivalence that is *either* actual *or* just possible, hence relative.

2. There is no possible difference between absolute equivalence that is *distinctly* both actual and just possible, hence generic, and absolute equivalence that is *indistinctly* both actual and just possible, hence general.

Still, only actual equivalence can contain any other equivalence: it can contain its own mere possibility, which conversely cannot contain its own actuality. Therefore, confusing between those equivalences requires the entirety of equivalence not only to be general, or indistinctly both actual and just possible, but also distinctly actual. Then:

1. The only form of *relative* equivalence left is that of an *indifferently relative or absolute, merely possible* equivalent. Hence Marx calling any just possible equivalence "the relative form of value"—as if it were alone or unilaterally all relativity:

   > The value of the linen [in "20 yards of linen = 1 coat"] is represented as relative value, or appears in relative form. [Mar67]

2. The only form of *equivalence* left is that of an *indifferently relative or absolute, already actual* equivalent. Hence Marx calling any actual equivalence "the equivalent form of value"—as if it were alone or unilaterally all equivalence:

   > The coat [in "20 yards of linen = 1 coat"] officiates as equivalent, or appears in equivalent form. [Mar67]

As thus, by mistaking actual equivalence for its mere possibility, one has only multiplicity left to both distinguish the actual, absolute equivalences of any omniequivalent from their also actual yet relative (single) selves and each of their converse just possible, absolute equivalences from its also just possible yet relative (single) self.[11]

Which in turn explains Marxian four progressive "forms of value":

---

[11] Hence the quantitative term "general" better qualifying an indistinctly both absolute and relative equivalence than the qualitative term "generic."

Form A

This is Marxian "elementary or accidental form of value." It mistakes actual equivalence for its mere possibility, which results in a single commodity being relative to its absolute equivalent:

> In the first form, 20 yds. [yards] of linen = 1 coat, it might, for ought that otherwise appears [despite appearances], be pure accident, that these two commodities are exchangeable in definite quantities. [Mar67]

Since relative equivalence always involves only two equivalents, it can only be a "pure accident," for excluding any other equivalence of either one of those equivalents: the only reason it "otherwise appears" is the confusion between absolute and relative equivalences.

Form B

This is Marxian "total or expanded form of value." It mistakes relative, merely possible equivalence for omniequivalence, which results in multiple commodities being relative, actual equivalents of an omniequivalent:

> In the second form, on the contrary, we perceive at once the background that determines, and is essentially different from, this accidental appearance. The value of the linen remains unaltered in magnitude, whether expressed in coats, coffee, or iron, or in numberless different commodities, the property of as many different owners. The accidental relation between two individual commodity-owners disappears. It becomes plain, that it is not the exchange of commodities which regulates the magnitude of their value; but, on the contrary, that it is the magnitude of their value which controls their exchange proportions. [Mar67]

Although it is true that equivalence will only lose its "accidental appearance" with multiple equivalences to the same equivalent, this is only true if those "numberless different" equivalences happen for the same owner, at the same time. Otherwise—if they only happen in different times or else for "as many different owners"—not even their infinite multiplicity could make them less "accidental" collectively than individually. However, there is no relative, actual equivalence of multiple commodities to the same relative, merely possible equivalent, for the same owner, at the same time: for that same owner, at that same time, any multiple, equivalent commodities must be absolute, merely possible equivalents of the same omniequivalent.

Form C

This is Marxian "general form of value," or "universal equivalent." It mistakes relative, actual equivalence for omniequivalence, which results in multiple commodities being relative, merely possible equivalents of an omniequivalent:

> The general form of relative value, embracing the whole world of commodities, converts the single commodity that is excluded from the rest, and made to play the part of equivalent—here the linen— into the universal equivalent. The bodily form of the linen is now the form assumed in common by the values of all commodities; it therefore becomes directly exchangeable with all and every of them. [Mar67]

However, the general equivalence (omniequivalence) of any commodity excludes only the *actual* equivalence of any other commodities: it still requires their merely possible equivalence—all commodities always "play the part of equivalent." Additionally, this merely possible equivalence to a general equivalent (to an omniequivalent) is—as already seen—*absolute*, rather than a "form of relative value."

Form D

This is Marxian "money-form." It mistakes individual for social omniequivalence:

> The universal equivalent form is a form of value in general. It can, therefore, be assumed by any commodity. On the other hand, if a commodity be found to have assumed the universal equivalent form (form C), this is only because and in so far as it has been excluded from the rest of all other commodities as their equivalent, and that by their own act. And from the moment that this exclusion becomes finally restricted to one particular commodity, from that moment only, the general form of relative value of the world of commodities obtains real consistence and general social validity.
>
> ...
>
> In passing from form A to form B, and from the latter to form C, the changes are fundamental. On the other hand, there is no difference between forms C and D, except that, in the latter, gold has assumed the equivalent form in the place of linen. [Mar67]

For Marx, omniequivalence consists in all inhabitants of "the world of commodities" excluding, "by their own act," a single commodity from among themselves. The reason is that, for mistaking absolute equivalence by any relative one, he cannot distinguish between the absolute equivalence of an individual omniequivalent—as required by whom individually handles its omniequivalence—and its relative equivalence—as required by whom owns its equivalents. Thus, he must confuse owning an individual omniequivalent with owning its equivalents. The result is an omniequivalent indistinguishable from all commodities, hence indistinctly owned by all commodity owners. This causes in turn the confusion between omniequivalence as not yet and already social, so the likewise indistinctly owned equivalents of any such omniequivalent must alone—as if unowned or even self-owned—"finally" distinguish themselves from their still nonsocial despite already "social" omniequivalent, thus making it always "excluded" from being each one of them.

Similarly, the whole truth of the value-forms B (total or expanded) and C (general or universal) can only be found in the combination of these two circumstances:

1. Individual omniequivalence alone requires the same commodities, at the same time, to be omniequivalents for some owners and relative, either actual or just possible equivalents for the others.

2. Mistaking an individual omniequivalent for a social one requires confusing among the perspectives of all commodity owners.

Let us consider an example. As below, E, F, and G are the moneyless owners of commodities x, y, and z (subscripted before the exchange and superscripted afterwards), respectively, of whom E wants y, F wants z, and G wants x. Then, let us choose E, who can only make this exchange possible by exchanging x for z with G as if already exchanging z for y with F, so z becomes E's individual omniequivalent (as asterisked):

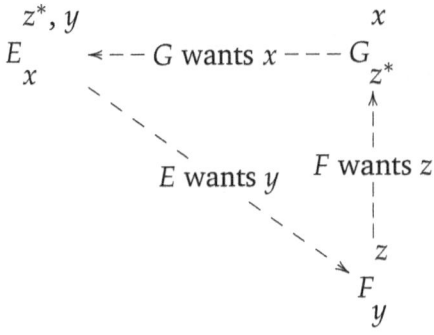

This way, z is an omniequivalent for E while being a relative, merely possible equivalent for G and a relative, actual equivalent for F. Thus:

1. Confusing between the perspectives of E and G makes z a relative, merely possible omniequivalent, as in form B (the "total or expanded" one).
2. Confusing between the perspectives of E and F makes z a relative, actual omniequivalent, as in form C (the "general" or "universal" one).

Yet relative, either actual or just possible equivalence is always individual, whether to commodity owners or to their commodities. Consequently, with Marx mistaking it for omniequivalence, he must find social omniequivalence elsewhere:

> Gold is in form D, what linen was in form C—the universal equivalent. The progress consists in this alone, that the character of direct and universal exchangeability—in other words, that the universal equivalent form—has now, by social custom, become finally identified with the substance, gold. [Mar67]

Still, what could it mean for a commodity to "finally" become a social form? Does money being gold mean that silver was never money? If another material becomes money by replacing gold with advantages, does this mean that gold was never money?

Such an obvious confusion between money and its representation (representational monetary identity), despite inadvertently reinforced by Marxian money-form, is what Marx himself simultaneously denounced as the "Fetishism" of commodities:

> What, first of all, practically concerns producers when they make an exchange, is the question, how much of some other product they get for their own? In what proportions the products are exchangeable? When these proportions have, by custom, attained a certain stability, they appear to result from the nature of the products, so that, for instance, one ton of iron and two ounces of gold appear as naturally to be of equal value as a pound of gold and a pound of iron in spite of their different physical and chemical qualities appear to be of equal weight.
>
> ...
>
> To what extent some economists are misled by the Fetishism inherent in commodities, or by the objective appearance of the social

> characteristics of labour, is shown, amongst other ways, by the dull and tedious quarrel over the part played by Nature in the formation of exchange value. Since exchange value is a definite social manner of expressing the amount of labour bestowed upon an object, Nature has no more to do with it, than it has in fixing the course of exchange. [Mar67]

Then, Marx blames representational monetary identity on exchange proportions that "have, by custom, attained a certain stability." As if prices were not constantly varying, sometimes catastrophically, without having the slightest effect on "the Fetishism inherent in commodities." However, and regardless of where the blame goes, why does he need to justify this confusion between money and its "physical and chemical qualities," whether such qualities belong to the price of a commodity—those "two ounces of gold"—or to the commodity thus priced—that "one ton of iron"? It is only because Marx unwittingly relies on the same confusion as a replacement for the social character that "as naturally" makes an otherwise individual omniequivalent money.

Still, how could any social omniequivalent (money) borrow its whole social character from a misrepresentation that presupposes it?

Handling individual omniequivalence requires remembering that an individual omniequivalent is a relative, either actual or just possible equivalent for the owners of its equivalents. On the contrary, mistaking an omniequivalent for its omniequivalence requires forgetting that instead it could be a relative, either actual or just possible equivalent for any commodity owner—including every omniequivalent owner—an oblivion only possible as long as one assumes this omniequivalent to be necessarily the same among all commodity owners, or necessarily *social* (money). So commodity "Fetishism" (representational monetary identity) and money (social omniequivalence) already share the same social character. Therefore, inherently fetishistic money requires just mistaking—as Marx always did—first an actual equivalent for a merely possible one (form A), then a relative, whether just possible or actual equivalent for an absolute one (respectively forms B and C), and finally an individual omniequivalent for a social one (form D). Whenever we make this last confusion, commodity owners become indistinguishable from each other, thus vanishing as exchange agents. Then, with only money and priced commodities left, representational monetary identity (commodity "Fetishism") cannot result from anything else: it becomes inherent in this money and its priced commodities.

Yet money does not itself cause our mistaking its representation for its identity: *we* do, by representing that identity as an object from the representation by which it is indistinguishable, despite no such object being inherently money. If gold or any other monetary representation were in itself necessarily money, *then*, and *only* then would commodity "Fetishism" be a necessary feature of all money and any priced commodities. Conversely, once a social omniequivalent is money but an individual one is not, money no longer needs to be "finally identified" with gold or any other monetary representation, although it still can—just before we finally overcome representational monetary identity.

Actual Money

Now, having understood social omniequivalence, we are finally able to define monetary identity as being social omniequivalence itself, and its representation as being whatever social omniequivalent we choose:

1. Social omniequivalence is the *identity* of money: the social equivalence between its representing object and all commodities.

2. A social omniequivalent is the *representation* of money: any object representing its own social omniequivalence or monetary identity.

However, what is the value of money: the value of its identity, that of its representation, both, or neither?

Monetary identity, as the social equivalence of a monetary representation (of an object representing money) to all its possible equivalents (to all commodities), is just an exchange value: it is the magnitude of an equivalence, by quantifying social omniequivalence. Consequently, the expression "money supply" cannot refer to monetary identity, except by confusing that social omniequivalence with its representing, socially omniequivalent object: money has in itself nothing of its own representation, whether as of a relative exchange value or as of an object. It is rather an absolute exchange value: the abstract magnitude of social omniequivalence. Thus, in its abstractness, money can only result from dividing the socially perceived exchange value of all commodities—which increases with commodity retention (by owners or third parties, or in transport delays)—by the socially perceived amount of monetary representation available—which decreases with money retention (by owners or third parties, or in transfer delays).

For example, with the social value of all commodities being 1,000,000 units of value and the social amount of monetary representation available being 1,000,000 grams of gold, a gram of gold represents one unit of value. This way, with the social amount of monetary representation available increasing 100% (from 1,000,000 to 2,000,000 grams of gold) without any change in the social value of all commodities (of 1,000,000 units of value), the magnitude of monetary identity *halves*, resulting in price *inflation* of 100%.

Conversely, no relative, objective exchange value could represent an absolute, abstract one without becoming as absolute and abstract as this represented monetary identity while both become a representational such identity. Hence, monetary identity (monetary value), unless representational, must exclude any other exchange value of its representing object.

Yet even when represented by an object with no relative exchange value, and whether distinct or not from that worthless representation, monetary identity still depends on exchange value. This is because it must always, or even only, result from dividing the exchange value society perceives all commodities to have by the amount of monetary representation society perceives is available. While its representing object must still confuse it with any relative exchange value in this object. Therefore, we can only understand monetary identity or its representation by first understanding exchange value as a general concept, independently of whether it quantifies a relative, primitive equivalence or an absolute, developed one.

Relative Exchange Value

Since being and nothingness are the same, the substitution of nothing by nothing must be, whether as everything or nothing, both everything and nothing. Otherwise, at least one (whichever) being, along with its (identical) nothingness, would not exist so neither any other (identical) nothingness nor all other (identical) beings would exist: neither being nor nothingness would exist, which is impossible. Thus, "omnistitution" means the absolute existence of the substitution of nothing by nothing, in the absolute impossibility of its nonexistence.

This way, since nothingness is the absolute existence of its own substitution by itself, it must be always different from itself: only this way can it substitute for itself, then remain identical to itself. Likewise, exchange value, which must (like anything else) be also its own substitutive nothingness, can only be identical to itself—as in relative equivalence—by being different from itself. Consequently, there is no relative equivalence between identical utilities or material qualities:

> Coats are not exchanged for coats, one use value is not exchanged for another of the same kind. [Mar67]

Still, since exchange value must be different from itself, relative equivalence is not even any partial identity between a pair of commodities—like their having a common weight. Otherwise, the necessary difference between their common exchange value and itself would make those two commodities also different from each other in any common set of material qualities, being thus no longer partially identical to each other.

Neither could relative equivalence, for the same reason, be any set of common *utilities* between those two commodities: although different commodities can share any single utility—as in their weights providing identical counterweights for a scale—all utilities depend on material qualities—like weight. Then, as the relative exchange value of any commodity already excludes its material qualities, it must likewise exclude its utilities, hence its common utilities with any other commodity.

> The utility of a thing makes it a use value. But this utility is not a thing of air. Being limited by the physical properties of the commodity, it has no existence apart from that commodity.
> ...
> As use-values, commodities are, above all, of different qualities, but as exchange-values they are merely different quantities, and consequently do not contain an atom of use-value. [Mar67]

Yet on the contrary, could exchange value be the common magnitude of *different* utilities or material qualities? If so, then how, since a common magnitude requires a common unit of measure, which in turn requires measuring a common object? How could different utilities or material qualities be identical quantities of the same object?

They obviously cannot, so exchange value could not result from utilities or material qualities, whether in their self-identity or self-difference. Then, what do we have left? What else could be the common exchange value between two different commodities, other than the common magnitude of identical or different utilities and material qualities? Which quantity—the magnitude of what—could be different from itself in two different commodities while still being identical to itself in either one of them as their common exchange value?

The only alternative left is the time interval taken to produce any commodity, which indeed can become, in different commodities, the same *quantity*, despite remaining, in each one of them, a different *process*, this way being, among those commodities, possibly different from itself. Consequently, the relative exchange value of any commodity, which makes it a relative equivalent, is just its common production-time interval with its relative, equivalent commodity.

This resembles the result arrived at by Marx, to whom the common exchange value between a pair of commodities was a shared quantity of "human labor in the abstract," which in turn was only measurable as a production-time interval:

> If then we leave out of consideration the use-value of commodities, they have only one common property left, that of being products of labor. But even the product of labor itself has undergone a change in our hands. If we make abstraction from its use-value, we make abstraction at the same time from the material elements and shapes that make the product a use-value; we see in it no longer a table, a house, yarn, or any other useful thing. Its existence as a material thing is put out of sight. Neither can it any longer be regarded as the product of the labor of the joiner, the mason, the spinner, or of any other definite kind of productive labor. Along with the useful qualities of the products themselves, we put out of sight both the useful character of the various kinds of labor embodied in them, and the concrete forms of that labor; there is nothing left but what is common to them all; all are reduced to one and the same sort of labor, human labor in the abstract.
>
> . . .

A use value, or useful article, therefore, has value only because human labor in the abstract has been embodied or materialized in it. How, then, is the magnitude of this value to be measured? Plainly, by the quantity of the value-creating substance, the labor, contained in the article. The quantity of labor, however, is measured by its duration, and labor time in its turn finds its standard in weeks, days, and hours. [Mar67]

Still, Marx's reasoning has these three flaws:

1. The material qualities of a useless commodity are no longer the material qualities of a commodity, but rather of just an object: although commodities depend on being useful, objects do not. So even when I leave "out of consideration the use-value of commodities," they can still have their material qualities to me—as useless objects. Conversely, only after having lost its material qualities, rather than just its utilities, "the product of labor itself has undergone a change in our hands": even while making "abstraction from its use-value," I am still free to make or not "abstraction at the same time from the material elements and shapes that make the product a use-value." Then, either "its existence as a material thing is put out of sight" or not, respectively, by me.

2. Different production processes can have different production-time intervals without having different products, if any—for example, one of them can yield more units of the same product than possibly any of the others in the same time interval, or yield fewer units, or just as many units, or else none at all. So even without considering "the useful qualities of the products themselves," nor thus—indeed—"the useful character of the various kinds of labor embodied in them," I can still consider "the concrete forms of that labor," as if those different labor forms had no useful product, but only different production-time intervals.

3. As a relative equivalent, the "product of labor" must always "be regarded as the product of the labor of the joiner, the mason, the spinner, or of any other definite kind of productive labor." Otherwise, its production-time interval would no longer be different from itself in its relative, equivalent commodity—as a different production process—this way no longer being identical to itself as another exchange value, nor being thus any longer the common exchange value between two different commodities.

Consequently, by "human labor in the abstract," Marx cannot yet mean the production-time interval that constitutes exchange value, even if almost doing so: with relative equivalence, that interval is not only abstract, as a quantity, but also concrete, as a process. Otherwise, it could not be, while still relative, both (qualitatively) different from itself—as a concrete production process—and (quantitatively) identical to itself—as an abstract interval magnitude. Any common exchange value between two directly equivalent commodities, for being just a shared production-time interval between them—one same time-interval magnitude of two different production processes—is always both abstract and concrete.

Monetary Value

In relative equivalence, one equivalent is just possible while the other is already actual. Then, with relative equivalence being just a shared production-time interval, the time interval taken to produce a relative, just possible equivalent is its own mere possibility of becoming its already actual self in its equivalent commodity. Still, no time interval could, either as one interval magnitude or two production processes, be both actual and just possible for the same commodity owner, at the same time. Nor could any production process be just possible while the magnitude of its own time interval is already actual for the same commodity owner, at the same time. Which leaves us no other choice: the *magnitude* of the time interval taken to produce a relative, just possible equivalent is the mere possibility of the already actual *process* of producing its relative, actual equivalent, for the same commodity owner, at the same time:

A	B
x: for A, the magnitude of the time interval taken to produce it is the mere possibility of the process of producing y	y: for B, the magnitude of the time interval taken to produce it is the mere possibility of the process of producing x

Conversely, the *process* of producing a relative, actual equivalent is the already actual *magnitude* of the time interval taken to produce its relative, just possible equivalent, for the same commodity owner, at the same time:

A	B
x: for B, the process of producing it is the already actual magnitude of the time interval taken to produce y	y: for A, the process of producing it is the already actual magnitude of the time interval taken to produce x

However, with omniequivalence, any omniequivalent object is not only an actual equivalent, but also a just possible one, by being itself all its multiple, just possible equivalents:

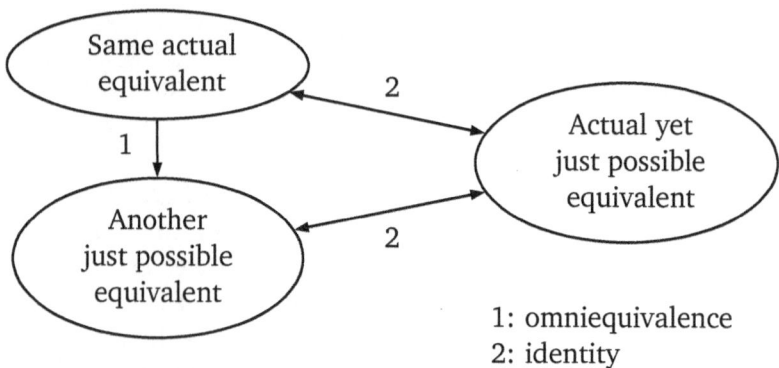

1: omniequivalence
2: identity

Therefore,

1. None of all just possible equivalents of an omniequivalent already has its own, actual production process, despite its indirect equivalence to each of the others: the whole exchange value of any of them is the magnitude of the time interval taken to produce it as the mere possibility of the process of producing their common, actual equivalent (omniequivalent).

2. Conversely, with an omniequivalent being itself all its equivalents:

   (a) The process of producing it must be identical to that of producing each one of those equivalents, being thus a variable production process.

   (b) The interval magnitude of the time taken to produce it must be identical to that of the time taken to produce each one of those equivalents, being thus a constant interval magnitude.

So the exchange value of an omniequivalent is both:

1. The variable process of producing each and all of its equivalents, which makes it both actual, as any single one of those processes, and just possible, as every other one of them.

2. The constant interval magnitude of the time taken to produce each and all of its equivalents, which makes it both actual, as any single one of those magnitudes, and just possible, as every other one of them.

Hence an omniequivalent object being both actual and just possible, which precisely makes it, along with all its included, constituting equivalents, absolute.

Still, if an omniequivalent must be, despite actual, rather just possible in its equivalents, it cannot yet be actual. While, if those equivalents must be, despite just possible, also actual in that omniequivalent, the same omniequivalent must already be actual. Yet how could an omniequivalent be both already and not yet actual at the same time, for the same, whether actual or just possible one of its owners? This can only happen when that omniequivalent is already *social* (money), with:

1. Actual money owners knowing their already owned social omniequivalent (money) to be just possible for at least one other, then just possible, money owner.

2. Merely possible money owners knowing their not yet owned social omniequivalent (money) to be already actual for at least one other, then actual, money owner.

Indeed, the buyer and the seller must be aware of each other. Both must know that, for the buyer—the actual money owner—money (the social omniequivalent) is actual as any of its equivalents it happens to be buying while, for the seller—the merely possible money owner—that money is just possible as every other one of its equivalents, which it does not happen to be buying.

Hence, with any omniequivalent being already social:

1. An individual (rather than social) omniequivalent does not yet have an omniequivalent exchange value: it can only represent the mere possibility of its own, social omniequivalence.

2. The actual exchange value of an individual (just possibly social) omniequivalent is the same one it has for the owners of its equivalents: that of a relative, either actual or just possible equivalence.

This way, the actual exchange value of an individual (not yet social) omniequivalent, for being that of its relative rather than absolute equivalence, has no means of properly expressing itself: its actual and just possible expressions exclude each other. As thus, individual (nonsocial) omniequivalents are just possibly omniequivalent since their omniequivalent exchange value is not yet actual while their actual exchange value has no means of properly expressing itself in an object. Only a socially omniequivalent object can be both actual and just possible at the same time, for the same, whether actual or just possible owner of that object—like the linen in this example:

> All commodities being equated to linen now appear not only as qualitatively equal as values generally, but also as values whose magnitudes are capable of comparison. By expressing the magnitudes of their values in one and the same material, the linen, those magnitudes are also compared with each other. For instance, 10 lbs [£10] of tea = 20 yards of linen, and 40 lbs of coffee = 20 yards of linen. Therefore, 10 lbs of tea = 40 lbs of coffee. [Mar67]

Additionally, since the process of producing a socially omniequivalent object is identical to that of producing each equivalent of its product, this omniequivalent-producing process is both actual, as that of producing any single equivalent of the same product, and just possible, as that of producing every other such equivalent. Hence, that socially omniequivalent object cannot have its own, definite production process because no such process could be always different from itself as required. All it has left is the common time-interval magnitude between the processes of producing any of all its equivalents and every other such equivalent, whether still common to its own production process or not:

1. A social omniequivalent must be *just an object*—even if one mistaken for its represented social omniequivalence—instead of also a *product*. So it is purely concrete, or objective.

2. Social omniequivalence itself must be *just an exchange value*—that of each and all of the equivalents of its representation—instead of belonging to a *product*. So it is purely abstract, or subjective.

Any relatively equivalent or individually omniequivalent object, on the contrary, must have a definite, either actual or just possible production process, this way alone being a relative, either actual or just possible equivalent, respectively: relatively valuable objects must be themselves either concrete production processes or the abstract magnitudes of their time intervals. Then, because no object could *represent* (not just be) an exchange value without being already distinct from—even if also mistaken for—it, any represented exchange value must be socially omniequivalent, for being conversely distinct from its representing object, and so from its relatively equivalent, definite production process. While:

1. Individual omniequivalence, for constituting a just possibly social omniequivalence, is never already represented.

2. Relative equivalence, for constituting an equivalent object of the definite production process of another, is not even representable.

This way:

1. Only a socially omniequivalent object represents an exchange value:

    (a) If actual (already social), then it already represents that exchange value.
    (b) If just possible (still individual), then it just possibly represents that exchange value.

Consequently:

1. With social omniequivalence:

    (a) Exchange value is purely abstract, or subjective, by having no definite, concrete production process.
    (b) Exchange value is both actual (to the buyer) and just possible (to the seller), or absolute.

2. With individual omniequivalence, either:

    (a) Exchange value is just possible, hence abstract, or subjective, as both a relative (just possible) equivalent and a social (just possible) omniequivalent.
    (b) Exchange value is actual but still concrete, or objective, as both a relative (actual) equivalent and an individual (actual) omniequivalent.

3. With relative equivalence, either:

    (a) Exchange value is just possible, hence abstract, or subjective, as both a relative (just possible) equivalent and an either (not yet) individual or (not yet) social omniequivalent.
    (b) Exchange value is actual but still concrete, or objective, as a relative (actual) equivalent, whether also as (already) an individual omniequivalent or not.

Or, in a diagram:

	Relative Equivalence	Individual Omni-equivalence	Social Omni-equivalence	
Actual	relative equivalent	relative equivalent, individual omni-equivalent	represen-tation	Concrete, objective
	–	–	exchange value	Abstract, subjective
Just possible	relative equivalent, individual omni-equivalent, social omni-equivalent	relative equivalent, social omni-equivalent	exchange value	Abstract, subjective

Hence Marx considering any exchange value as purely abstract: his mistaking both relative equivalence and individual omniequivalence for money (for social omniequivalence) forces him to reduce a resulting indifferently abstract or concrete exchange value to a purely abstract one (to social omniequivalence). Finally, by uncritically accepting representational monetary identity, which mistakes any object representing money for the purely abstract exchange value of that money, Marx turns even this object into the same pure abstraction of its monetary value, without ever noticing, each time, how impure that abstraction has then become.

Monetary Representation

Money, like everything else, is the substitution of nothing by nothing. However, that substitution is also the absence of any substitution, being thus the same nothingness either substituted or substitutive in it. Then, despite remaining the whole substitution of nothing by nothing:

1. Money must be just the substitutive nothingness.

2. Money must be just the substituted nothingness.

Indeed, there can be no substitutive nothingness without a substituted yet identical one. Likewise, conversely, there can be no substituted nothingness without a substitutive yet identical one. Hence, by being just an either substituted or substitutive nothingness, money *represents* its own *identity* to the whole substitution of nothing by nothing: it is a monetary *representation* of monetary *identity*.

Still, the substitutive nothingness always includes the substituted one, by remaining the same nothingness for which it already substitutes. Consequently, whenever substitutive and because already so, nothingness remains also substituted, hence in itself the identity between an either substitutive or substituted nothingness and the whole substitution of nothing by nothing. So any substitutive monetary representation can be called *representational monetary identity*—a monetary representation from which monetary identity becomes indistinguishable.

While the substituted nothingness, on the contrary, always excludes the substitutive one, by not yet being its own substitutive, actual self. Consequently, whenever substituted but not substitutive, nothingness must not yet in itself be the identity between an either substituted or substitutive nothingness and the whole substitution of nothing by nothing. Even then, it still represents that identity, by remaining the same as its own substitutive nothingness, hence also their whole substitution: the substituted nothingness is already an actual representation of its own identity, despite not yet in itself being already actual. How is that possible?

A representation can simultaneously be *not yet* and *already* actual only by being its own, *just actual* representation, or *metarepresentation*. A just actual representation is anything depending on always representing whatever it already represents, which must in turn be not yet actual, or it would become its own representation, thus making that representation also just possible. For example, any word must be a just actual representation of its meaning. Nothing can be a word—and not just its noise—without representing this meaning, which conversely must remain a represented, just possible meaning, or it would become that same word—so the written or spoken sound of, say, "everything" would itself already *be* everything, instead of *meaning* it. In contrast, gold is *not* a just actual representation of money since gold *can* exist without representing money: similarly to money, gold is both actual and just possible, which precisely makes it indistinguishable from the money it represents.[12]

Still, which monetary representation could be—as a word is—already actual without being also just possible?

The mere possibility of a word is already that word as a just actual representation of its just possible meaning, being thus merely possible only as that meaning, and so identical to it, which hence is already actual for conversely being that same word. Indeed, no just actual representation could have a mere possibility other than its represented one. Neither could it no longer be possible, so any just actual representation is always identical to the mere possibility thus represented, which yet remains a *represented possibility*, despite as also a *representing actuality*: nothing could be just its own representation. So any just actual representation of (just possible) money can also represent its own identity to that money without ever becoming indistinguishable from it.

Public-Key Cryptography

For example, let us imagine a public rule by which, somehow, the number zero publicly represents the number nine only privately to me. Under that rule, the number zero publicly becomes a just actual representation of any just possible number, which is the actual number nine only privately to me—to whom alone the number nine conversely represents the number zero. Hence, that same rule is a just actual, public representation (by zero) of a converse just possible, private one (of zero by nine).

So a generalized such rule could publicize the representation of any private number (like nine) by a public one (like zero) without conversely publicizing the representation of this public (the zero-like) number by that private (the nine-like) one. Public-key cryptography does precisely that: it uses two keys—two numbers—mathematically related in such a way that, although either key can only represent the other, only the private one can reveal its represented key. Then:

1. Using the public key to encrypt any content results in another content that only a holder of the private key can decrypt.

2. Using the private key to sign any content results in another content that every holder of the public key can authenticate.

---

[12]This indistinction was precisely what Marx called commodity "Fetishism."

The Bitcoin monetary system uses public-key cryptography to build *signature chains*, each link of which representing a *coin transfer*:

> Each owner transfers the coin to the next by digitally signing a hash [a numeric representation] of the previous transaction and the public key of the next owner and adding these to the end of the coin. [Nak09]

Then, money becomes a privately signed yet public chain of monetary transactions despite never becoming itself public. Indeed, whenever socially represented by pairs of a private and the corresponding public keys, money must either be possible—but not yet actual—as each private monetary key, or actual—but no longer possible—as the corresponding public monetary key. So any such cryptographic, public-key monetary representation is a *metarepresentation* of money.

Metamoney

Finally, since a substituted, just possible representation is purely abstract, or merely subjective, the private ownership of any *metarepresented money*, or *metamoney*—like Bitcoin—is no longer the private holding of an object, but rather the private *knowledge* of its just possible, substituted representation—in Bitcoin, the ownership of its private key.

Hence the necessarily decentralized nature of any form of metamoney (like Bitcoin): the existence of a central metamonetary authority would require money owners to share every monetary representation, whether just possible or just actual (in Bitcoin, every private or public key, respectively) at least with that authority. So preventing the same authority from owning all money—all just possible monetary representations (in Bitcoin, all private keys)—would require proxy representations of this money (metamoney) to be privately owned by all its original owners. However, any proxy metamoney must itself be metamonetary, being thus a just actual representation of a just possible representation of money. Consequently, for being just possible, any metarepresented monetary representation is indistinguishable from a then also just possible since just possibly represented money. So its proxy representation must rather be a proxy representational identity of that money: whenever centralized, metamoney loses its actual representation to its then-representational monetary identity.[13]

---

[13]The Canadian money MintChip is precisely this proxy representation of a centralized, never-yet actual metarepresentation of money—a representational, falsely metamonetary identity.

Representational Monetary Value

As long as representational monetary identity mistakes a monetary object—say, gold—for its represented money, any relative, either actual or just possible exchange value of that object *replaces* its true monetary value, or *substitutes* for its absolute, both actual and just possible equivalence to all commodities. While conversely, the identity of its represented money becomes a representational exchange value as either:

1. The substitution of monetary value by a relative, *actual* exchange value, so the monetary object, as thus any priced commodity, falsely becomes in itself money. This is Marxian "Fetishism" of money and priced commodities.

2. The substitution of monetary value by a relative, *just possible* exchange value, so the monetary object falsely becomes each one of all its just possible equivalents. This is the "price of money."

However, which money could have no true monetary value?

Anything substitutive must be actual—even if also just possible—by being the nothingness that already substitutes for itself. Conversely, anything substituted must be just possible, by being the nothingness that does not yet substitute for itself. Finally, any representing object must be already substitutive of whatever it represents. This way, whenever an object representing money has a relative exchange value in addition to its represented, absolute one, this absolute, substituted exchange value becomes the mere possibility of its own relative, substitutive self.

Likewise, the substituted nothingness must be the whole possibility of the substitutive one, so a represented exchange value is the whole possibility of any other exchange value representing it. Consequently, no exchange value could represent a monetary value smaller than itself, except after losing part of its own possibility, hence after decreasing.

Nor could any exchange value represent a monetary value of which the magnitude is identical to its own since:

1. The substituted nothingness must be different from the substitutive one.

2. Exchange values—whether monetary or not—can only differ in their magnitudes.

Then, only the monetary value of a relatively worthless object has any possible magnitude: a relatively valuable object can only represent a greater monetary value than its own, relative exchange value.

Yet representational monetary identity, despite any relative exchange value of the monetary object being smaller than its absolute, represented monetary value, must still mistake that relative exchange value for this absolute one. Then, representational monetary value, as just any relative exchange value mistaken for a greater monetary value than itself, must have an ever greater magnitude:

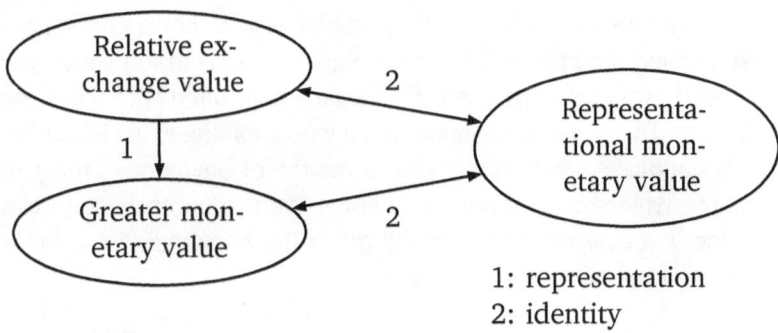

1: representation
2: identity

Conversely, for such a relative, representational monetary value to represent a greater monetary value than itself:

1. It must be both a monetary value and its representation.

2. It must represent itself as already greater than itself.

Finally, a monetary value must be a liability to represent a greater exchange value than itself. Indeed, only an owed, interest-paying monetary value can be a greater amount of represented money than of its representation, this way becoming ever more money. So representational monetary value must become a *debt*.

Therefore, once the object representing the absolute exchange value of money has also its own, relative exchange value, representational monetary identity, otherwise unnoticeable, becomes rather noticeable. This happens both subjectively—privately—as money mistaken by greed, and objectively—publicly—as money mistaken by debt.[14]

---

[14]Confusing both debt and greed with money results in also confusing between debt and greed. Then, debt (greed) necessarily motivates credit, whether credit conversely motivates debt or not.

Fractional-Reserve Banking

We are now ready to understand not only how, but also *why* fractional-reserve banking originated.

> It started with goldsmiths. As early bankers, they initially provided safekeeping services, making a profit from vault storage fees for gold and coins deposited with them. People would redeem their "deposit receipts" whenever they needed gold or coins to purchase something, and physically take the gold or coins to the seller who, in turn, would deposit them for safekeeping, often with the same banker. Everyone soon found that it was a lot easier simply to use the deposit receipts directly as a means of payment. These receipts, which became known as notes, were acceptable as money since whoever held them could go to the banker and exchange them for metallic money. [Nic94]

For people to deposit their gold with others and still own it in the form of deposit receipts, these receipts must conversely represent that deposited gold, with any such gold becoming the same as its representing receipts. Indeed, the substituted—represented—nothingness (gold) and the substitutive—representing—one (gold-deposit receipts) must be the same. As thus, a relatively worthless object can only represent money by being itself directly monetary, which is impossible if its monetary value belongs to another object—in a rather *indirect* monetary representation. Then, only as a relative exchange value could any object represent the monetary value of a different object than itself, so monetary gold-deposit receipts must be valuable independently of representing gold money, by having their own, relative exchange value.

Conversely, no relatively valuable object could represent a relatively worthless monetary one, which would then itself be directly—rather than indirectly represented as—money. Hence, the monetary gold represented by gold-deposit receipts must also have its own, relative exchange value—independently of being money. Finally, since any exchange value can only represent a greater one than itself, those gold-deposit receipts must have a relative exchange value smaller than that of the gold they represent, which in turn must have a smaller one than its represented monetary value. However, in their nothingness, all those exchange values must still be the same as each other, by sharing an either actual (fetishistic) or just possible (self-pricing) monetary self. Consequently, whenever we create any proxy representations of money, representational monetary identity becomes (at least remains) a representational monetary value—so any gold-deposit receipts representing monetary gold must represent ever more money, or an interest-paying debt:

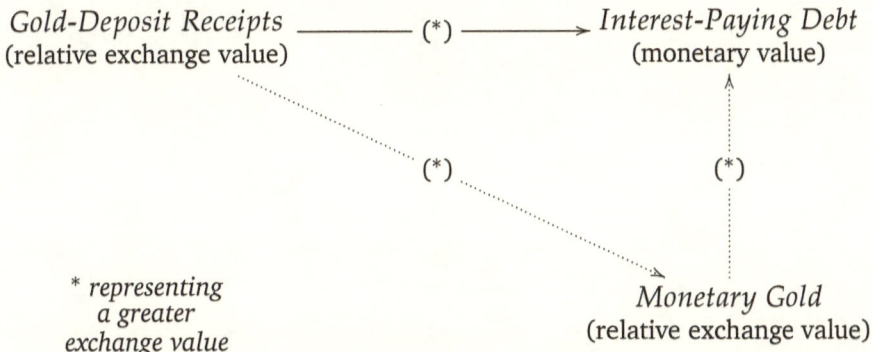

Indeed, with receipts for deposited gold replacing that gold as money, the same gold can only have its actual, ever-increasing monetary value in those receipts. Additionally, as each gold-deposit receipt always depends on a gold deposit, its excess monetary value becomes a gold-deposit fee. Finally, as deposited gold is a mere possibility, which has in its receipts its whole actuality, the actual gold in deposit can be a fraction of itself as represented in those receipts, or even absent. So eventually, deposit receipts for monetary gold become just debt, on which deposit fees become just interest, whether the owners of those receipts are aware of this or not: fractional-reserve banking becomes possible.

Yet why would it become actual?

A self-increasing, representational monetary value is purely abstract, or subjective, being thus also limitless, or infinite. Then, its recursive increase must overcome any concrete, objective limits—any costs of producing and maintaining this monetary system—with only and both:

1. Ever cheaper actual monetary representations: additional proxy representations of monetary gold must be cheaper than the legacy ones they transitionally represent.

2. Ever smaller fractions of actual gold in deposit: represented gold must be just possible, which makes actual gold in deposit strictly unnecessary.

The result is fractional-reserve banking: money becomes debt while its representation becomes ever cheaper—even if already digital.[15]

---

[15] It is almost as if Moore's law were a fractional-reserve banking law.

Conclusion

Once money becomes debt, the social money supply must recursively expand. Yet it must expand not only as a monetary representation, but also as its misrepresented monetary identity, hence as the monetary value—the socially perceived exchange value of all commodities divided by the socially perceived money supply—for which it mistakes its own self-expanding self. So monetary value must falsely expand, whether in currency and commercial markets, as the greedy "Fetishism" respectively of money and priced commodities,[16] or in financial markets, as the greedy "price of money"—money as future (asset) prices. The result is:

1. Representational monetary value increasing relatively to its true monetary value: monetary identity deflation—an increase of monetary value (including that of assets) driven by the representational identity of money.

2. Representational monetary value eventually reverting to its true monetary value: price inflation—a decrease of monetary value (including that of assets) driven by the true value of money.

This is the system of monetary crisis, also known as the "boom-and-bust" cycle, in which monetary identity deflation is the "boom" and price inflation is the "bust."

Additionally, as the social money supply recursively expands, it also causes the scale of this representational identity cycle to expand in both its false increase of monetary value and the corresponding inflationary "correction." Eventually, one of the resulting money devaluations, cumulative or not, must prevent an amount of debt-principal redemptions or even interest payments large enough to reduce the proportion of credit,

---

[16]When exchanged for different money, a social omniequivalent reverses back into an individual, just possible one as an either bought or sold actual commodity. Then, if representational, its just possible monetary identity becomes rather actual as that same commodity, hence as the "Fetishism" of either bought or sold money.

hence of the social money supply, to the social exchange value of all commodities. This is the third and last moment of the same cycle: *price deflation*, or a "credit crunch"—a true increase of monetary value.

So a true monetary deflation eventually results from the sufficiently prolonged alternation between some falsely deflationary and inflationary moments in the cycle of representational monetary value. After which, if still (or already) possible, the whole cycle resumes:

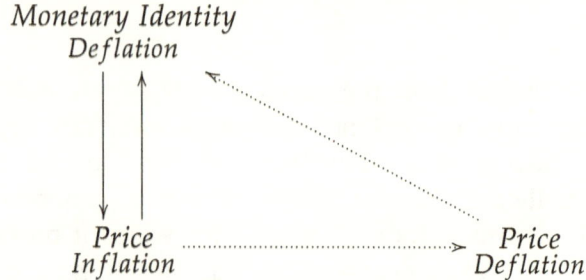

Finally, how can we avoid such an erratic, systemic cycle of permanent monetary crisis? Since that cycle results, at each moment, from the representational identity of money, overcoming it requires a monetary system that inherently distinguishes monetary identity from its representation: a metamonetary system, like Bitcoin.

Bibliography

[Mar67] Karl Marx. *Capital: A Critique of Political Economy*, volume I, chapter 1. 1867. Translated by Samuel Moore and Edward Aveling. Edited by Friedrich Engels. Marxists Internet Archive (http://www.marxists.org/archive/marx/works/1867-c1/).

[Nak09] Satoshi Nakamoto. *Bitcoin: A Peer-to-Peer Electronic Cash System*. 2009. Bitcoin home (http://bitcoin.org/bitcoin.pdf).

[Nic94] Dorothy M. Nichols. *Modern Money Mechanics*. 1994. Written in 1961. Revised in 1968, 1975 and 1992. Author's copy (http://omniequivalence.com/modern-money-mechanics/).

www.ingramcontent.com/pod-product-compliance
Lightning Source LLC
Chambersburg PA
CBHW021922170526
45157CB00005B/2147